Arsenal

THE
KINGS
OF
CARDIFF

Arsenal

THE
KINGS
OF
CARDIFF

hamlyn

Acknowledgements
The publisher would like to thank Craig Stevens and Julian Flanders at
Butler and Tanner. Stuart MacFarlane, Josh James and Joe Cohen at Arsenal.

Words *Joshua James*

Produced for Hamlyn by Butler and Tanner Ltd

First published in 2005 by Hamlyn
a division of Octopus Publishing Group Ltd
2-4 Heron Quays, London E14 4JP

ISBN 0 600 61469 7

A CIP catalogue record for this book is available from the British Library

Printed and bound in the UK by Butler and Tanner Ltd

10 9 8 7 6 5 4 3 2 1

Executive Editor *Trevor Davies*
Project Editor *Julian Flanders at Butler and Tanner*
Design *Butler and Tanner*
Production *Martin Croshaw*
All images Copyright © Arsenal Football Club Plc/Stuart MacFarlane/David Price

Contents

Foreword
The Manager's View

We won our third FA Cup in four years in May 2005, and although I admit we didn't play with our usual style and attacking power against Manchester United, the important thing was to return to Highbury with the cup.

The fact that we did so was down to a tremendous mental belief, excellent teamwork, and a strong determination and desire to win. All of our penalties were excellently taken – credit to the five players because they all showed great confidence and courage to take the kicks.

The feeling of winning the FA Cup in such dramatic circumstances, and celebrating the win with the Arsenal fans, is hard to describe, but it was a great end to the season.

When I look back at our four finals at the Millennium Stadium, I have to say that ironically, our best performance came in the 2001 final against Liverpool – the only time we lost. There were extraordinary circumstances that day that prevented us from winning, but perhaps the disappointment we felt at the final whistle has helped us to win subsequent finals there.

The following year we beat Chelsea to win the first half of the 'double' – we scored two fantastic goals that day, and perhaps that's when we started to love the Millennium Stadium.

Against Southampton in 2003 we were under big, big pressure to win the cup, because we had lost the league and we needed to end the season with a trophy.

It was a similar situation last season. We were determined to end the season on a high, and we did that.

When you look at the list of clubs we have knocked out of the FA Cup over the past five years or so it's amazing. We have beaten everyone in the competition. We've beaten the big teams like Manchester United, Chelsea, Newcastle, Tottenham and Liverpool, and a lot of them away from home. We've also had to beat a lot of lower league teams and often they have been just as difficult, if not more difficult to beat, than the Premiership teams because they give absolutely everything when they play Arsenal. We are a big trophy for teams like that so I'm proud of the way my players have been professional and taken every game seriously. The cup has also given the opportunity to a lot of our younger players to experience intense competition, and I believe this has been to their great benefit.

I've got many personal highlights from the FA Cup. There's no doubt that there's a special atmosphere for these games, even more so at Highbury, and the longer a cup run lasts, the more work you put in and the more you want to win the trophy.

It's difficult to say why we've had such a good record in this competition since I've been here, and to be honest I can't believe that I've been to five finals now.

But we love the FA Cup at this club, every year it's a big aim for us.

We will be sorry to leave the Millennium Stadium behind, but equally we have a big determination to play in the first FA Cup Final at the new Wembley Stadium.

Arsène Wenger

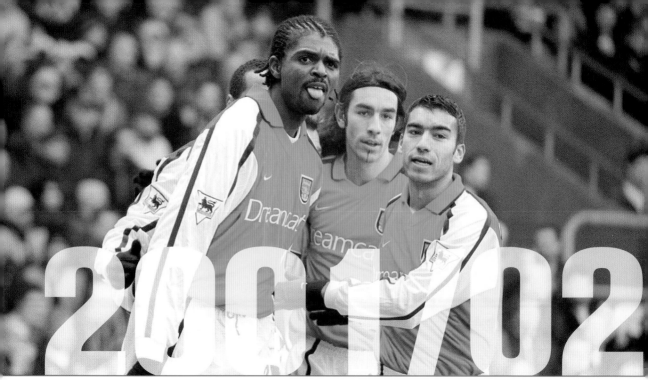

Third Round Vicarage Road
2001/02

2 WATFORD Noel-Williams 13, Gayle 90

4 ARSENAL Henry 8, Ljungberg 10, Kanu 63, Bergkamp 84

Right **Kanu** soars above the home defence to powerfully head home as Arsenal's cup campaign starts with a comprehensive defeat of Watford. The Nigerian converted from Patrick Vieira's cross for Arsenal's third goal at Vicarage Road.

WATFORD

13 Alec **CHAMBERLAIN**   2 Patrick **BLONDEAU**   6 Ramon **VEGA**   28 Pierre **ISSA**
29 Neil **COX**   7 Allan **NIELSEN**   25 Gary **FISKEN**   4 Paolo **VERNAZZA**   27 Marcus **GAYLE**
9 Tommy **SMITH**   15 Gifton **NOEL-WILLIAMS**   Substitutes   1 Espen **BAARDSEN**
36 Jamie **HAND** (Vernazza) 90   34 Lloyd **DOYLEY**   18 Heidar **HELGUSON** (Fisken) 78
12 Nordin **WOOTER**

ARSENAL

13 Stuart **TAYLOR**   22 Oleg **LUZHNY**   5 Martin **KEOWN**   23 Sol **CAMPBELL**   3 Ashley **COLE**
8 Fredrik **LJUNGBERG**   4 Patrick **VIEIRA**   16 Giovanni **VAN BRONCKHORST**
7 Robert **PIRES**   25 **KANU**   14 Thierry **HENRY**   Substitutes   43 Graham **STACK**
20 Matthew **UPSON**   18 Gilles **GRIMANDI**   10 Dennis **BERGKAMP** (Kanu) 82
11 Sylvain **WILTORD** (Henry) 82

Fourth Round Highbury
2001/02

1	**ARSENAL** Bergkamp 28
0	**LIVERPOOL**

Above **Giovanni van Bronckhorst** slides in to dispossess Emile Heskey in a keenly-fought Fourth Round encounter at Highbury. Arsenal were intent on laying the ghost of the previous year's Cup Final defeat to Liverpool just eight months earlier.

ARSENAL

24 Richard **WRIGHT**   22 Oleg **LUZHNY**   23 Sol **CAMPBELL**   5 Martin **KEOWN**
3 Ashley **COLE**   11 Sylvain **WILTORD**   4 Patrick **VIEIRA**   16 Giovanni **VAN BRONCKHORST**
7 Robert **PIRES**   10 Dennis **BERGKAMP**   14 Thierry **HENRY**   Substitutes
43 Graham **STACK**   2 Lee **DIXON**   20 Matthew **UPSON** (Wiltord) 68   18 Gilles **GRIMANDI**
(van Bronckhorst) 84   15 Ray **PARLOUR** (Pires) 20

LIVERPOOL

12 Jerzy **DUDEK**   29 Stephen **WRIGHT**   4 Sami **HYYPIA**   2 Stephane **HENCHOZ**
23 Jamie **CARRAGHER**   8 Emile **HESKEY**   17 Steven **GERRARD**   16 Dietmar **HAMANN**
18 John Arne **RIISE**   9 Nicolas **ANELKA**   10 Michael **OWEN**   Substitutes
19 Pegguy **ARPHEXAD**   21 Gary **McALLISTER**   13 Danny **MURPHY** (Wright) 80
15 Patrik **BERGER**   37 Jari **LITMANEN** (Anelka) 46

Above **Dennis Bergkamp beats Jamie Carragher to the ball to head the only goal of the game at the far post.**

Right **The Dutchman turns away to celebrate in front of the Clock End after glancing home from Thierry Henry's centre. The goal was just reward as Arsenal had forced the early pace, despite losing Robert Pires through injury in the 20th minute.**

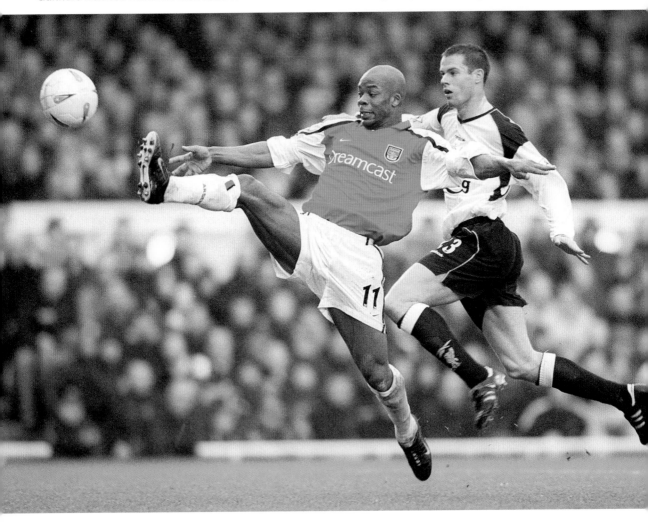

5 ARSENAL Wiltord 38, 81, Kanu 50, Adams 67, Parlour 88
2 GILLINGHAM King 47, Gooden 54

Bottom Right Thierry Henry slaloms past visiting defender Barry Ashby during Arsenal's entertaining 5–2 destruction of the Gills. Returning after five months out injured, skipper Tony Adams had made it 3–2 after Gillingham had twice equalised.

ARSENAL

24 Richard **WRIGHT** 2 Lee **DIXON** 6 Tony **ADAMS** 23 Sol **CAMPBELL** 57 **JUAN**
11 Sylvain **WILTORD** 4 Patrick **VIEIRA** 15 Ray **PARLOUR** 17 **EDU** 25 **KANU**
9 Francis **JEFFERS** Substitutes 1 David **SEAMAN** 26 Igors **STEPANOVS**
18 Gilles **GRIMANDI** (Kanu) 75 7 Robert **PIRES** (Jeffers) 63 14 Thierry **HENRY** (Edu) 63

GILLINGHAM

1 Vince **BARTRAM** 2 Mark **PATTERSON** 5 Barry **ASHBY** 18 Chris **HOPE**
26 David **PERPETUINI** 21 Simon **OSBORN** 4 Paul **SMITH** 12 Paul **SHAW**
11 Ty **GOODEN** 9 Marlon **KING** 19 Iffy **ONUORA** Substitutes 6 Guy **BUTTERS**
7 Nayron **NOSWORTHY** 8 Andy **HESSENTHALER** (Osborn) 77 14 Marcus **BROWNING**
(Gooden) 78 10 Guy **IPOUA** (Onuora) 78

Arsenal 5   Gillingham 2   17

Sixth Round St James' Park
2001/02

1   **NEWCASTLE UNITED**   Robert 52
1   **ARSENAL**   Edu 14

Above The Gunners travelled to St James' Park for the Quarter-Final clash and took the lead through Edu from close range. But then Arsenal, without a host of first-team regulars, were left hanging on for the replay after Laurent Robert's second-half equaliser.

NEWCASTLE UNITED

1 Shay **GIVEN**   18 Aaron **HUGHES**   5 Andy **O'BRIEN**   34 Nikos **DABIZAS**
24 Sylvain **DISTIN**   4 Nolberto **SOLANO**   6 Clarence **ACUNA**   22 Jamie **McCLEN**
32 Laurent **ROBERT**   9 Alan **SHEARER**   16 Carl **CORT**   Substitutes   13 Steve **HARPER**
3 Robbie **ELLIOTT**   23 Shola **AMEOBI** (Cort) 70   20 Lomana Tresor **LUA LUA**
35 Olivier **BERNARD**

ARSENAL

24 Richard **WRIGHT**   2 Lee **DIXON**   26 Igors **STEPANOVS**   23 Sol **CAMPBELL**
12 **LAUREN**   8 Fredrik **LJUNGBERG**   18 Gilles **GRIMANDI**   4 Patrick **VIEIRA**   17 **EDU**
11 Sylvain **WILTORD**   25 **KANU**   Substitutes   1 David **SEAMAN**   27 Stathis **TAVLARIDIS**
7 Robert **PIRES** (Ljungberg) 58   10 Dennis **BERGKAMP** (Edu) 61   28 Kolo **TOURE**

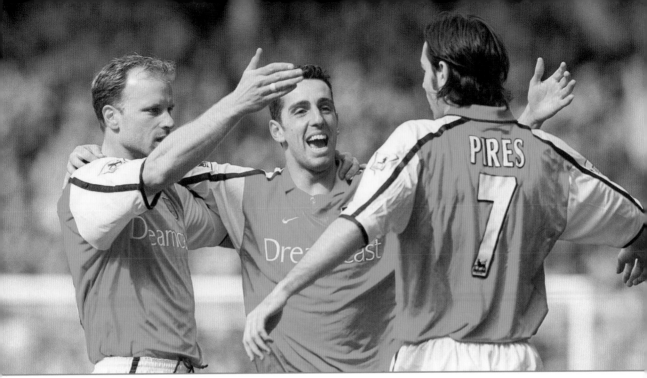

Sixth Round Replay Highbury
2001/02

3 ARSENAL Pires 2, Bergkamp 9, Campbell 50
0 NEWCASTLE UNITED

Above Robert Pires celebrates the opener with Edu and man-of-the-match Dennis Bergkamp. The goal was to be Pires' last contribution to the campaign as he suffered a cruciate ligament injury later in the first-half. By that stage of the season though, he had already done enough to earn the Football Writers' Player of the Year Award.

ARSENAL

24 Richard **WRIGHT** 22 Oleg **LUZHNY** 6 Tony **ADAMS** 23 Sol **CAMPBELL** 3 Ashley **COLE** 8 Fredrik **LJUNGBERG** 4 Patrick **VIEIRA** 17 **EDU** 7 Robert **PIRES** 10 Dennis **BERGKAMP** 11 Sylvain **WILTORD** Substitutes 1 David **SEAMAN** 2 Lee **DIXON** (Wiltord) 77 18 Gilles **GRIMANDI** (Pires) 27 25 **KANU** 9 Francis **JEFFERS** (Edu) 69

NEWCASTLE UNITED

1 Shay **GIVEN** 18 Aaron **HUGHES** 5 Andy **O'BRIEN** 34 Nikos **DABIZAS** 24 Sylvain **DISTIN** 4 Nolberto **SOLANO** 6 Clarence **ACUNA** 8 Kieron **DYER** 32 Laurent **ROBERT** 9 Alan **SHEARER** 16 Carl **CORT** Substitutes 13 Steve **HARPER** 3 Robbie **ELLIOTT** (Distin) 84 25 Brian **KERR** (Acuna) 83 20 Lomana Tresor **LUA LUA** (Cort) 84 35 Olivier **BERNARD**

Arsenal 3   Newcastle United 0   21

Semi-Final Old Trafford
2001/02

1 ARSENAL Festa og 39
0 MIDDLESBROUGH

Above **Thousands of expectant Arsenal fans turn their end of Old Trafford gold for the FA Cup Semi-Final. It was their second trip to the venue for a semi-final in consecutive seasons.**

ARSENAL

24 Richard **WRIGHT** 12 **LAUREN** 5 Martin **KEOWN** 23 Sol **CAMPBELL** 22 Oleg **LUZHNY** 11 Sylvain **WILTORD** 4 Patrick **VIEIRA** 17 **EDU** 8 Fredrik **LJUNGBERG** 10 Dennis **BERGKAMP** 14 Thierry **HENRY** Substitutes 1 David **SEAMAN** 2 Lee **DIXON** (Luzhny) 32 15 Ray **PARLOUR** (Campbell) 58 25 **KANU** (Bergkamp) 89 9 Francis **JEFFERS**

MIDDLESBROUGH

1 Mark **SCHWARZER** 27 Robbie **STOCKDALE** 17 Ugo **EHIOGU** 6 Gareth **SOUTHGATE** 37 Franck **QUEUDRUE** 31 Luke **WILKSHIRE** 14 Michael **DEBEVE** 7 Robbie **MUSTOE** 32 Allan **JOHNSTON** 20 Dean **WINDASS** 11 Alen **BOKSIC** Substitutes 25 Mark **CROSSLEY** 5 Gianluca **FESTA** (Ehiogu) 32 28 Colin **COOPER** 24 Phil **STAMP** (Wilkshire) 56 23 Carlos **MARINELLI** (Johnston) 76

Below **Thierry Henry wriggles his way between three Boro players as the two teams battle for supremacy in the early stages.**

Above After surviving a couple of scares of their
own, it was Arsenal who made the breakthrough
late in the first-half. Thierry Henry's whipped-in
corner was diverted into his own net off the shin
of the unfortunate Gianluca Festa (obscured).

Right **Thierry Henry displays typical poise and balance as Arsenal began to take control in the second-half. They searched for the killer second, and came close through Dennis Bergkamp and Sylvain Wiltord, but had to be content with a 1–0 victory.**

Right After playing a major part in helping to narrowly see off the challenge of Middlesbrough, Sol Campbell, in his first season at the Club, celebrates reaching the FA Cup Final with a delighted Edu.

Final Millennium Stadium
2001/02

2 ARSENAL Parlour 70, Ljungberg 80
0 CHELSEA

Above Needing only a draw from their next league game to wrap up the title, Arsène Wenger's men went into the 2002 FA Cup Final hoping to become the first team ever to win the 'double' by winning the FA Cup half first. On a glorious summer afternoon the Arsenal fans descended on the Millennium Stadium in Cardiff for the second consecutive May.

ARSENAL

1 David SEAMAN 12 LAUREN 23 Sol CAMPBELL 6 Tony ADAMS 3 Ashley COLE
11 Sylvain WILTORD 15 Ray PARLOUR 4 Patrick VIEIRA 8 Fredrik LJUNGBERG
10 Dennis BERGKAMP 14 Thierry HENRY Substitutes 24 Richard WRIGHT
2 Lee DIXON 5 Martin KEOWN (Wiltord) 90 17 EDU (Bergkamp) 72 25 KANU (Henry) 81

CHELSEA

23 Carlo CUDICINI 15 Mario MELCHIOT 6 Marcel DESAILLY 13 William GALLAS
3 Celestine BABAYARO 30 Jesper GRONKJAER 8 Frank LAMPARD 17 Emmanuel PETIT
14 Graeme LE SAUX 22 Eidur GUDJOHNSEN 9 Jimmy Floyd HASSELBAINK
Substitutes 1 Ed DE GOEY 26 John TERRY (Babayaro) 46 10 Slavisa JOKANOVIC
11 Boudewijn ZENDEN (Melchiot) 77 25 Gianfranco ZOLA (Hasselbaink) 68

Arsenal 2   Chelsea 0   31

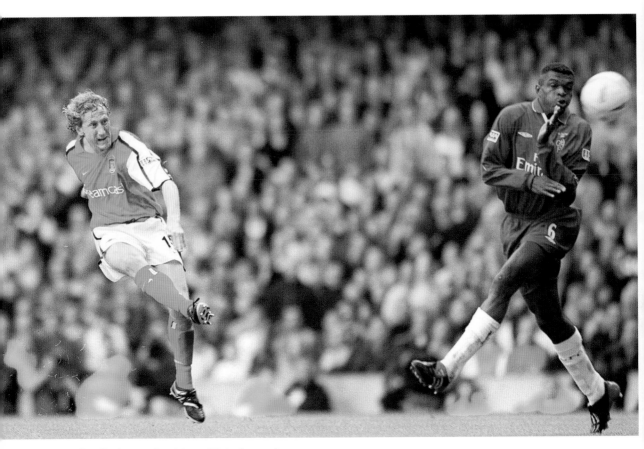

Above Ray Parlour writes himself into Arsenal folklore with a stunning long-range goal to give Arsenal the lead in the second-half. There appeared to be little danger when he picked up the ball, but he advanced unopposed before lashing home past Carlo Cudicini.

Ray Parlour celebrates after putting Arsenal ahead against Chelsea and on the way to a famous victory.

Left and Below Ten minutes from time Freddie Ljungberg makes the game safe with his own Cup Final classic. Shrugging off the challenge of John Terry, the scampering Swede then looked up before sending home a curling shot from the edge of the area.

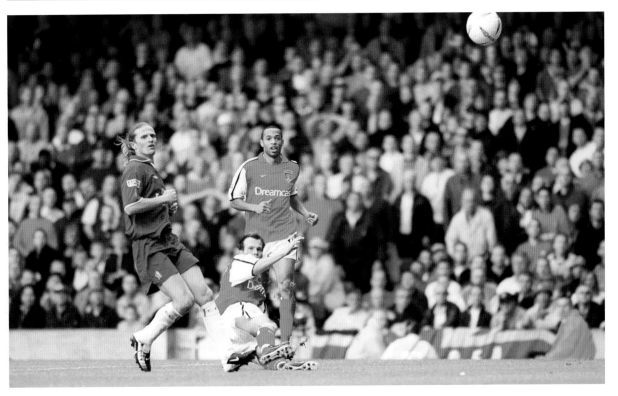

Above Freddie is overjoyed after becoming the first player to score in consecutive FA Cup Finals since Tottenham's Bobby Smith in 1961 and 1962. Unlike the previous year though, his afternoon would have a happy ending as he, Thierry Henry and Sylvain Wiltord all begin their collection of FA Cup Winners' medals with the Club.

Above and Right **With the Cup**
now back in Arsenal's
possession once more, the
celebrations can begin in
earnest at the Millennium
Stadium. Club captain Tony
Adams, and his deputy so often
throughout the season, Patrick
Vieira, hoist the famous old
trophy together – the eighth
time the Gunners have had
their name engraved on
the Cup.

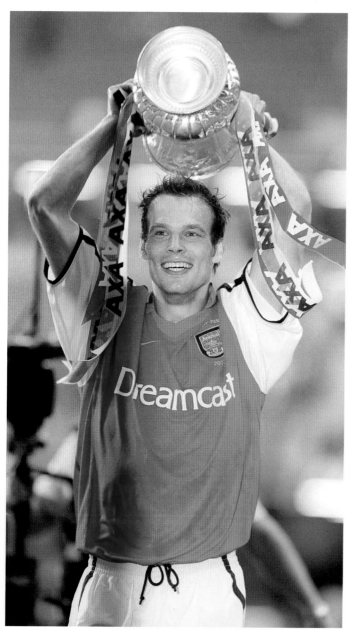

Left and Above **Man of the moment Freddie Ljungberg gets his hands on the silverware,** while David Seaman, Sylvain Wiltord and Patrick Vieira enjoy that winning feeling.

Right and Below **The two scorers proudly show off the fruits of their labour while back in the dressing room Sol Campbell, Thierry Henry, Ashley Cole and Patrick Vieira get to grips with the Cup in the north dressing room at the Millennium Stadium.**

Far Right **Arsène Wenger – the first Arsenal manager to win the FA Cup on more than one occasion.**

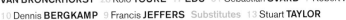

2 ARSENAL Bergkamp 15, McNiven og 67
0 OXFORD UNITED

Above Dennis Bergkamp becomes only the 15th player to score 100 goals for Arsenal, bringing up his ton in the win over a plucky Oxford United side as the Gunners begin their defence of the Cup with a 2–0 home win.

ARSENAL

1 David SEAMAN 22 Oleg LUZHNY 5 Martin KEOWN 20 Matthew UPSON 31 Giovanni VAN BRONCKHORST 28 Kolo TOURE 17 EDU 31 Sebastian SVARD 7 Robert PIRES 10 Dennis BERGKAMP 9 Francis JEFFERS Substitutes 13 Stuart TAYLOR 26 Igors STEPANOVS 19 GILBERTO (Svard) 77 35 David BENTLEY (Toure) 77 11 Sylvain WILTORD (Bergkamp) 80

OXFORD UNITED

1 Andy WOODMAN 2 Scott McNIVEN 11 Matthew ROBINSON 5 Andy CROSBY 6 David WATERMAN 18 Matthew BOUND 4 David SAVAGE 21 Bobby FORD 27 Roy HUNTER 22 David OLDFIELD 23 Steve BASHAM Substitutes 28 Abdu SALL 12 Dean WHITEHEAD 10 Andrew SCOTT (Savage) 64 17 Jefferson LOUIS (Oldfield) 54 9 Lee STEELE (Basham) 84

Fourth Round Highbury
2002/03

1	**FARNBOROUGH TOWN** Baptiste 71
5	**ARSENAL** Campbell 19, Jeffers 23, 68, Bergkamp 74, Lauren 79

On a truly unique occasion at Highbury, Arsenal are technically the away side, hence the blue kit, after non-Leaguers Farnborough were originally drawn at home but switched the tie to North London. The Gunners averted any threat of a giant-killing though, with a comfortable 5–1 win.

FARNBOROUGH TOWN

1 Tony **PENNOCK**   10 Christian **LEE**   24 Darren **ANNON**   5 Nathan **BUNCE**
3 Justin **GREGORY**   16 Danny **CARROLL**   20 Gary **HOLLOWAY**
7 Steve **WATSON**   2 Michael **WARNER**   22 Rocky **BAPTISTE**   18 Ken **CHARLERY**
Substitutes   11 Tony **TAGGART**   19 Gary **BUTTERWORTH** (Charlery) 80
8 Lenny **PIPER** (Carroll) 86   14 Chris **PIPER** (Holloway) 76   9 Joff **VANSITTART**

ARSENAL

13 Stuart **TAYLOR**   12 **LAUREN**   23 Sol **CAMPBELL**   18 Pascal **CYGAN**
16 Giovanni **VAN BRONCKHORST**   7 Robert **PIRES**   15 Ray **PARLOUR**
4 Patrick **VIEIRA**   28 Kolo **TOURE**   25 **KANU**   9 Francis **JEFFERS**
Substitutes   1 David **SEAMAN**   22 Oleg **LUZHNY**   17 **EDU** (Kanu) 76
10 Dennis **BERGKAMP** (Pires) 66   11 Sylvain **WILTORD** (Toure) 66

Fifth Round Old Trafford
2002/03

0 MANCHESTER UNITED

2 ARSENAL Edu 35, Wiltord 52

Right Edu's free-kick takes a deflection en route, but finds the back of the net to set Arsenal on their way to a superb 2–0 Fifth Round win at Old Trafford.

Including Semi-Final wins, it was Arsenal's third win at the venue in the FA Cup in three seasons – a fourth was to follow just a matter of months later.

MANCHESTER UNITED

1 Fabien **BARTHEZ** 2 Gary **NEVILLE** 6 Rio **FERDINAND** 24 Wes **BROWN** 27 Mikael **SILVESTRE** 7 David **BECKHAM** 16 Roy **KEANE** 18 Paul **SCHOLES** 20 Ole Gunnar **SOLSKJAER** 11 Ryan **GIGGS** 10 Ruud **VAN NISTELROOY** Substitutes 19 **RICARDO** 3 Phil **NEVILLE** 22 John **O'SHEA** 8 Nicky **BUTT** (Beckham) 83 21 Diego **FORLAN** (Giggs) 71

ARSENAL

1 David **SEAMAN** 12 **LAUREN** 5 Martin **KEOWN** 23 Sol **CAMPBELL** 3 Ashley **COLE** 15 Ray **PARLOUR** 4 Patrick **VIEIRA** 17 **EDU** 7 Robert **PIRES** 11 Sylvain **WILTORD** 9 Francis **JEFFERS** Substitutes 20 Guillaume **WARMUZ** 18 Pascal **CYGAN** 16 Giovanni **VAN BRONCKHORST** (Pires) 84 28 Kolo **TOURE** (Wiltord) 90 14 Thierry **HENRY** (Jeffers) 73

Above and Far Right **Sylvain Wiltord maintains his scoring record at Old Trafford, and his affection for the FA Cup in general, with Arsenal's second soon after the re-start.** Once the two-goal lead was established the midfield duo of Patrick Vieira and Edu then took over to dominate possession and offer the hosts no route back into the game.

Left **Less than a year after the title was clinched away to Manchester United, David Seaman celebrates another famous victory at Old Trafford, as the Gunners win the battle of the top two teams in the league to progress to the last eight of the FA Cup.**

2 ARSENAL Jeffers 36, Henry 45
2 CHELSEA Terry 3, Lampard 84

Above Francis Jeffers, an ever-present in the starting line-up in the run to the Final, salutes the fans after grabbing the 36th-minute equaliser in a dramatic, pulsating Quarter-Final clash with Chelsea.

ARSENAL

1 David **SEAMAN**   12 **LAUREN**   23 Sol **CAMPBELL**   5 Martin **KEOWN**
16 Giovanni **VAN BRONCKHORST**   15 Ray **PARLOUR**   4 Patrick **VIEIRA**   17 **EDU**
8 Fredrik **LJUNGBERG**   14 Thierry **HENRY**   9 Francis **JEFFERS**
Substitutes 20 Guillaume **WARMUZ**   18 Pascal **CYGAN**   28 Kolo **TOURE** (Henry) 78
7 Robert **PIRES** (Ljungberg) 64   11 Sylvain **WILTORD** (Jeffers) 64

CHELSEA

23 Carlo **CUDICINI**   15 Mario **MELCHIOT**   13 William **GALLAS**   26 John **TERRY**
3 Celestine **BABAYARO**   30 Jesper **GRONKJAER**   8 Frank **LAMPARD**   17 Emmanuel **PETIT**
20 Jody **MORRIS**   25 Gianfranco **ZOLA**   9 Jimmy Floyd **HASSELBAINK**
Substitutes 35 Rhys **EVANS**   29 Robert **HUTH**   21 Enrique **DE LUCAS** (Gronkjaer) 72
11 Boudewijn **ZENDEN** (Zola) 46   22 Eidur **GUDJOHNSEN** (Petit) 72

Above and Right **Undoubtedly one of the goals of the competition in 2003. Set free by an incisive through-ball from Patrick Vieira, Thierry Henry completely bamboozled Carlo Cudicini, spinning past him with a 360° turn, before stroking the ball home. The goal came just moments after Henry had side-footed an effort against the post, and 25 minutes after he had seen his penalty saved by Cudicini.**

Above and Right **Arsenal made most of the running in this cup tie which ebbed and flowed at a frantic pace, and at times Arsène Wenger's side were at their dangerous best. But they failed to kill off the game and there was a late twist when Frank Lampard stabbed home an equaliser with five minutes remaining.**

Arsenal, however, were still in the Cup, and still dreaming of a possible 'treble', although now they had surrendered home advantage in this fascinating Quarter-Final duel.

Sixth Round Replay Stamford Bridge
2002/03

1	**CHELSEA**	Terry 79
3	**ARSENAL**	Terry og 24, Wiltord 34, Lauren 82

Above **Skipper Patrick Vieira,** albeit hampered with a knee injury, led by example with an immense performance in midfield to help ten-man Arsenal to a memorable win at Stamford Bridge and book a place in the Semi-Finals. The talismanic Frenchman set-up Arsenal's first two goals, then maintained possession in the second-half when Chelsea were threatening to make a comeback.

CHELSEA

23 Carlo **CUDICINI**   15 Mario **MELCHIOT**   26 John **TERRY**   13 William **GALLAS**
12 Mario **STANIC**   8 Frank **LAMPARD**   20 Jody **MORRIS**   17 Emmanuel **PETIT**
14 Graeme **LE SAUX**   25 Gianfranco **ZOLA**   9 Jimmy Floyd **HASSELBAINK**
Substitutes   1 Ed **DE GOEY**   6 Marcel **DESAILLY**   30 Jesper **GRONKJAER** (Stanic) 35
11 Boudewijn **ZENDEN** (Morris) 46   22 Eidur **GUDJOHNSEN** (Petit) 59

ARSENAL

13 Stuart **TAYLOR**   12 **LAUREN**   23 Sol **CAMPBELL**   18 Pascal **CYGAN**
28 Kolo **TOURE**   15 Ray **PARLOUR**   4 Patrick **VIEIRA**   17 **EDU**   7 Robert **PIRES**
11 Sylvain **WILTORD**   9 Francis **JEFFERS**   Substitutes   20 Guillaume **WARMUZ**
16 Giovanni **VAN BRONCKHORST** (Jeffers) 68   8 Fredrik **LJUNGBERG** (Pires) 74
10 Dennis **BERGKAMP**   14 Thierry **HENRY** (Wiltord) 75

Above   After weaving past a couple of Chelsea defenders Lauren
unleashes a left-foot rocket to make it 3–1 and settle the nerves
for the travelling fans. Arsenal went into the replay without
Ashley Cole, David Seaman and Martin Keown, and with Freddie
Ljungberg, Dennis Bergkamp and Thierry Henry all on the bench,
but yet again they proved too strong for Chelsea – making it
13 consecutive games unbeaten against their London rivals.

Far Right   Following Pascal Cygan's dismissal in the 66th minute,
Kolo Toure shone after being moved to centre-half. It was the
first time the Ivorian had played there for the Gunners, hitherto
having been used as a full-back or midfield utility man, but his
impressive display in the heart of the back four for the last half-
hour was a sign of things to come in his Gunners career.

TheFA CUP

1 ARSENAL   Ljungberg 34
0 SHEFFIELD UNITED

Above **Another season, another trip to Old Trafford to watch Arsenal in the FA Cup Semi-Final. The league leaders, chasing an unprecedented second consecutive League and FA Cup 'double', were hot favourites against Division One side Sheffield United, but the encounter was closer than many anticipated.**

ARSENAL

1 David **SEAMAN**   12 **LAUREN**   5 Martin **KEOWN**   23 Sol **CAMPBELL**   3 Ashley **COLE**   15 Ray **PARLOUR**   4 Patrick **VIEIRA**   17 **EDU**   8 Fredrik **LJUNGBERG**   11 Sylvain **WILTORD**   9 Francis **JEFFERS**   Substitutes   13 Stuart **TAYLOR**   22 Oleg **LUZHNY**   19 **GILBERTO** (Vieira) 56   10 Dennis **BERGKAMP** (Wiltord) 81   14 Thierry **HENRY** (Jeffers) 66

SHEFFIELD UNITED

23 Paddy **KENNY**   36 John **CURTIS**   2 Rob **KOZLUK**   6 Robert **PAGE**   17 Phil **JAGIELKA**   7 Michael **BROWN**   8 Stuart **MCCALL**   18 Michael **TONGE**   16 Peter **NDLOVU**   34 Steve **KABBA**   14 Wayne **ALLISON**   Substitutes   24 Gary **KELLY**   5 Shaun **MURPHY**   12 Nick **MONTGOMERY** (Allison) 60   9 Carl **ASABA** (McCall) 60   10 Paul **PESCHISOLIDO** (Kabba) 79

Arsenal 1   Sheffield United 0   65

Right **Sylvain Wiltord demonstrates ample athleticism and keeps his eye on the ball to retain possession.**

Above **Francis Jeffers seems to be on a collision course with Stuart McCall's boot as the two battle for the ball.**

Arsenal were by no means at their best in the Semi-Final, and were made to work hard for the entire 90 minutes by Neil Warnock's Blades.

Left **Scrappy and controversial it may have been, but Freddie Ljungberg's goal in the first-half ensured that Arsenal would be at the FA Cup Final for the third year in succession.**

Referee Graham Poll inadvertently checked the progress of United midfielder Michael Tonge by colliding with him, and later in the same move Ljungberg poked the ball home off the underside of the crossbar after Sylvain Wiltord's shot had rebounded against the post.

Above The highlight of the game was not a goal, but this remarkable, instinctive, match-winning save by David Seaman. In his 1,000th senior fixture, the 39-year-old somehow kept out Paul Peschisolido's close range effort just in front of the line, when the ball was already past him. This incredible piece of agility, with just five minutes remaining, saw Arsenal through to the Final.

Left Patrick Vieira, who handed the captain's armband to David Seaman after being taken off injured, congratulates the goalkeeper on a stunning piece of goalkeeping.

Final Millennium Stadium
2002/03

1 ARSENAL Pires 38
0 SOUTHAMPTON

Due to persistent rain in the run-up to the game, the roof on the Millennium Stadium was kept closed during the 2003 Final, meaning the two teams lined up for the first ever FA Cup Final played 'indoors'.

With Patrick Vieira injured, David Seaman, playing what was to prove his final game for the Club, led the team out behind Arsène Wenger.

ARSENAL

1 David **SEAMAN**   12 **LAUREN**   5 Martin **KEOWN**   22 Oleg **LUZHNY**   3 Ashley **COLE**
8 Fredrik **LJUNGBERG**   15 Ray **PARLOUR**   19 **GILBERTO**   7 Robert **PIRES**
10 Dennis **BERGKAMP**   14 Thierry **HENRY**   Substitutes 13 Stuart **TAYLOR**
28 Kolo **TOURE**   16 Giovanni **VAN BRONCKHORST**   11 Sylvain **WILTORD** (Bergkamp) 77
25 **KANU**

SOUTHAMPTON

14 Antti **NIEMI**   32 Chris **BAIRD**   5 Claus **LUNDEKVAM**   11 Michael **SVENSSON**
3 Wayne **BRIDGE**   33 Paul **TELFER**   8 Matt **OAKLEY**   12 Anders **SVENSSON**
4 Chris **MARSDEN**   36 Brett **ORMEROD**   9 James **BEATTIE**   Substitutes 1 Paul **JONES**
(Niemi) 66   6 Paul **WILLIAMS**   20 Danny **HIGGINBOTHAM**   29 Fabrice **FERNANDES**
(Baird) 86   21 Jo **TESSEM** (A Svensson) 75

Arsenal 1   Southampton 0   73

Left Southampton's Claus Lundekvam resorts to desperate measures in an attempt to stop Thierry Henry sprinting clean through on goal.

Player of the Season Henry was immediately into the thick of the action, and could have given Arsenal the lead after just 30 seconds. Indeed he forced three saves out of Antti Niemi in the opening 20 minutes or so.

Above The ever-reliable Robert Pires strikes home the only goal of the game with seven minutes of the first-half remaining.

Dennis Bergkamp sent the ball into the middle, Freddie Ljungberg couldn't convert but Pires was lurking and he made no mistake with his right foot.

Arsenal 1   Southampton 0   75

Below **Chris Baird and Michael Svensson are powerless to stop Robert Pires striking the ball home from eight yards out.**

Right Dennis Bergkamp
shields the ball from Claus
Lundekvam. Having been in the
position of holding a one-goal
lead in the FA Cup Final two
years earlier, only to see the
game cruelly snatched away
from them in the dying
moments, the Arsenal players
were determined that history
would not repeat itself. In the
closing stages they were more
interested in protecting their
slender lead than looking for
a second.

Far Right The final whistle
sounds and it's smiles all
round as Kolo Toure and
Thierry Henry kick off the
celebrations while the Arsenal
fans fill the air with a rendition
of '1–0 to the Arsenal'.

Arsenal 1   Southampton 0   79

The injured Patrick Vieira and goalkeeper David Seaman lift the trophy in unison as the streamers and fireworks are released.

The title may have eluded them, but Arsenal would not be relinquishing their grip on the FA Cup – becoming the first team to retain the trophy for 20 years and making it nine wins in all in the competition – second highest in the all-time list.

Right David Seaman ended his Arsenal career in fitting style – with a clean sheet and a trophy. It was his 564th and final appearance in Arsenal's colours, and he was collecting his ninth major honour.

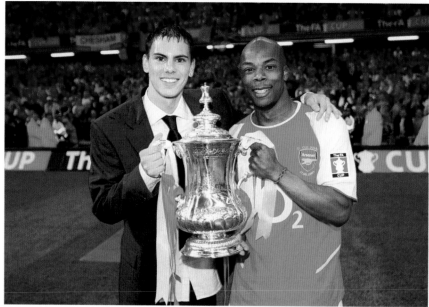

Once again the Arsenal players show they know how to celebrate as Freddie Ljungberg cracks open the bubbly while Kolo Toure shows off his spectacular routine of flips and somersaults.

2004/05

2 ARSENAL Reyes 50, van Persie 70
1 STOKE CITY Thomas 45

A young Arsenal team were forced to come from behind to see off Championship side Stoke City in the Third Round at Highbury.

After falling behind on the stroke of half-time, José Antonio Reyes smashed in the equaliser (above) before Robin van Persie, on his FA Cup debut, flicked home the winner.

ARSENAL

1 Jens **LEHMANN** 27 Emmanuel **EBOUE** 28 Kolo **TOURE** 20 Philippe **SENDEROS** 22 Gael **CLICHY** 21 Jermaine **PENNANT** 15 Francesc **FABREGAS** 4 Patrick **VIEIRA** 7 Robert **PIRES** 9 José Antonio **REYES** 11 Robin **VAN PERSIE** Substitutes 24 Manuel **ALMUNIA** 31 Justin **HOYTE** (Eboue) 71 18 Pascal **CYGAN** 39 Sebastian **LARSSON** 42 Quincy **OWUSU-ABEYIE**

STOKE CITY

15 Steve **SIMONSEN** 2 Wayne **THOMAS** 32 Gerry **TAGGART** 22 Lewis **BUXTON** 16 Marcus **HALL** 17 Darel **RUSSELL** 19 Chris **GREENACRE** 21 John **HALLS** 3 Clive **CLARKE** 10 Ade **AKINBIYI** 27 Jason **JARRETT** Substitutes 1 Ed **DE GOEY** 7 Carl **ASABA** (Greenacre) 77 9 Gifton **NOEL-WILLIAMS** 2 Karl **HENRY** (Halls) 52 4 John **EUSTACE** (Clarke) 77

Arsenal 2   Stoke City 1   87

2 **ARSENAL** Vieira 53 pen, Ljungberg 82

0 **WOLVERHAMPTON WANDERERS**

Above Right **Patrick Vieira** maintains his concentration to slot home from the penalty spot and send Arsenal on their way to a comfortable Fourth Round victory. The captain stepped up after Thierry Henry had been fouled in the box and Freddie Ljungberg later added a second to extend the Gunners' incredible unbeaten home record in the FA Cup to 19 matches.

ARSENAL

1 Jens **LEHMANN**   27 Emmanuel **EBOUE**   23 Sol **CAMPBELL**   18 Pascal **CYGAN**
22 Gael **CLICHY**   8 Fredrik **LJUNGBERG**   4 Patrick **VIEIRA**   16 Mathieu **FLAMINI**
9 José Antonio **REYES**   11 Robin **VAN PERSIE**   14 Thierry **HENRY**
Substitutes 24 Manuel **ALMUNIA**   31 Justin **HOYTE**   42 Quincy **OWUSU-ABEYIE**
(Ljungberg) 84   15 Francesc **FABREGAS** (van Persie) 76   7 Robert **PIRES** (Reyes) 70

WOLVERHAMPTON WANDERERS

1 Michael **OAKES**   5 Joleon **LESCOTT**   6 Jody **CRADDOCK**   20 Joachim **BJORKLUND**
7 Shaun **NEWTON**   4 Seyi **OLOFINJANA**   8 Paul **INCE**   11 Mark **KENNEDY**   3 Lee **NAYLOR**
19 Ki-Hyeon **SEOL**   27 Carl **CORT**   Substitutes 15 Kevin **COOPER**   24 Keith **ANDREWS**
16 Kenny **MILLER** (Bjorklund) 61   33 Leon **CLARKE** (Olofinjana) 76   10 Colin **CAMERON**
(Ince) 86

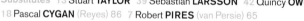

Fifth Round Highbury
2004/05

| 1 | **ARSENAL** Pires 78 |
| 1 | **SHEFFIELD UNITED** Gray 90 pen |

Above For the third game in a row, Arsenal were drawn at home to Championship opponents, but Sheffield United proved tough opposition for an Arsenal starting line-up which contained no Englishmen.

Robert Pires tucked home the opener after Paddy Kenny spilled Mathieu Flamini's shot but a last-minute Andy Gray penalty ensured a replay at Bramall Lane.

ARSENAL

24 Manuel **ALMUNIA**   27 Emmanuel **EBOUE**   28 Kolo **TOURE**   20 Philippe **SENDEROS**
22 Gael **CLICHY**   8 Fredrik **LJUNGBERG**   15 Francesc **FABREGAS**   16 Mathieu **FLAMINI**
9 José Antonio **REYES**   10 Dennis **BERGKAMP**   11 Robin **VAN PERSIE**
Substitutes   13 Stuart **TAYLOR**   39 Sebastian **LARSSON**   42 Quincy **OWUSU-ABEYIE**
18 Pascal **CYGAN** (Reyes) 86   7 Robert **PIRES** (van Persie) 65

SHEFFIELD UNITED

1 Paddy **KENNY**   14 Jon **HARLEY**   4 Nick **MONTGOMERY**   15 Paul **THIRLWELL**
6 Phil **JAGIELKA**   7 Andy **LIDDELL**   17 Leigh **BROMBY**   18 Michael **TONGE**
32 Danny **CULLIP**   26 Derek **GEARY**   8 Andy **GRAY**   Substitutes   12 Alan **QUINN**
10 Danny **CADAMARTERI**   21 Jonathan **FORTE** (Montgomery) 82   30 Paul **SHAW**
(Thirlwell) 45   16 Simon **FRANCIS** (Liddell) 82

Arsenal 1   Sheffield United 1   91

Fifth Round Replay Bramall Lane
2004/05

0 SHEFFIELD UNITED
0 ARSENAL

**ARSENAL WON 4–2
ON PENALTIES**

Sheffield United : Gray scored, Jagielka scored, Quinn saved, Harley saved
Arsenal: Lauren scored, Vieira scored, Ljungberg scored, Cole scored

Right A night of high-drama was eventually settled only on penalties as an inexperienced Arsenal side failed to breakthrough the resilient Blades team during the 120 minutes.

Manuel Almunia proved to be the hero, saving two penalties in the shoot-out as all four Arsenal penalty takers found the back of the net.

SHEFFIELD UNITED

1 Paddy **KENNY** 26 Derek **GEARY** 5 Chris **MORGAN** 17 Leigh **BROMBY** 14 Jon **HARLEY**
7 Andy **LIDDELL** 4 Nick **MONTGOMERY** 6 Phil **JAGIELKA** 15 Paul **THIRLWELL**
18 Michael **TONGE** 8 Andy **GRAY** Substitutes 16 Simon **FRANCIS** 19 Steve **KABBA**
30 Paul **SHAW** 33 Danny **HAYSTEAD** 12 Alan **QUINN** (Tonge) 97

ARSENAL

24 Manuel **ALMUNIA** 12 **LAUREN** 20 Philippe **SENDEROS** 18 Pascal **CYGAN**
3 Ashley **COLE** 16 Mathieu **FLAMINI** 4 Patrick **VIEIRA** 15 Francesc **FABREGAS**
22 Gael **CLICHY** 40 Arturo **LUPOLI** 8 Fredrik **LJUNGBERG**
Substitutes 13 Stuart **TAYLOR** 28 Kolo **TOURE** (Fabregas) 90 27 Emmanuel **EBOUE**
30 Jeremie **ALIADIERE** (Flamini) 113 42 Quincy **OWUSU-ABEYIE** (Lupoli) 45

Sheffield United 0   Arsenal 0   93

Sixth Round The Reebok Stadium
2004/05

0 BOLTON WANDERERS
1 ARSENAL Ljungberg 3

Above The FA Cup had become Arsenal's only realistic hope of silverware and the team needed to show all of their fighting spirit after Ljungberg nipped in to score after just three minutes at the Reebok Stadium.

The team defended stoically to preserve the clean sheet, and Ljungberg should have capped the win in the final minute but somehow contrived to miss when it appeared easier to score from five yards with the goal at his mercy.

BOLTON WANDERERS

22 Jussi **JAASKELAINEN** 18 Nicky **HUNT** 5 Bruno **N'GOTTY** 26 Ben **HAIM**
11 Ricardo **GARDENER** 4 Kevin **NOLAN** 20 Fernando **HIERRO** 6 Gary **SPEED**
7 Stelios **GIANNAKOPOULOS** 21 El-Hadji **DIOUF** 14 Kevin **DAVIES**
Substitutes 1 Kevin **POOLE** 16 Ivan **CAMPO** 15 Radhi **JAIDI** (Hunt) 68
9 Henrik **PEDERSEN** (Haim) 81 23 Vincent **CANDELA** (Hierro) 68

ARSENAL

1 Jens **LEHMANN** 12 **LAUREN** 28 Kolo **TOURE** 20 Philippe **SENDEROS**
22 Gael **CLICHY** 8 Fredrik **LJUNGBERG** 4 Patrick **VIEIRA** 16 Mathieu **FLAMINI**
7 Robert **PIRES** 9 José Antonio **REYES** 10 Dennis **BERGKAMP**
Substitutes 13 Stuart **TAYLOR** 3 Ashley **COLE** 11 Robin **VAN PERSIE**
15 Francesc **FABREGAS** 27 Emmanuel **EBOUE**

Bolton Wanderers 0   Arsenal 1   95

3	**ARSENAL** Pires 42, van Persie 86, 90
0	**BLACKBURN ROVERS**

This year saw an earlier trip than usual to Wales, as both Semi-Finals were played in Cardiff. In their record-breaking 25th FA Cup Semi-Final appearance, Arsenal survived an early physical onslaught from Rovers before taking the lead through Robert Pires late in the first-half.

The challenges continued to be full-blooded though and it wasn't until substitute Robin van Persie scored twice in the last five minutes that another appearance in the Cup Final was certain.

ARSENAL

1 Jens **LEHMANN**   12 **LAUREN**   28 Kolo **TOURE**   20 Philippe **SENDEROS**   3 Ashley **COLE** 4 Patrick **VIEIRA**   19 **GILBERTO**   7 Robert **PIRES**   8 Fredrik **LJUNGBERG** 9 José Antonio **REYES**   10 Dennis **BERGKAMP**   Substitutes   24 Manuel **ALMUNIA** 18 Pascal **CYGAN**   15 Francesc **FABREGAS** (Ljungberg) 50   11 Robin **VAN PERSIE** (Bergkamp) 82   30 Jeremie **ALIADIERE** (Reyes) 89

BLACKBURN ROVERS

1 Brad **FRIEDEL**   2 Lucas **NEILL**   24 Andy **TODD**   15 Aaron **MOKOENA**   29 Ryan **NELSEN** 22 Dominic **MATTEO**   12 Morten Gamst **PEDERSEN**   5 Garry **FLITCROFT**   18 Steven **REID** 20 David **THOMPSON**   10 Paul **DICKOV**   Substitutes   13 Peter **ENCKELMAN** 8 Kerimoglu **TUGAY**   9 Jon **STEAD** (Matteo) 83   7 Brett **EMERTON** (Flitcroft) 51 31 Robbie **SAVAGE** (Thompson) 63

Below Philippe Senderos, growing in stature as
an Arsenal centre-half with each appearance,
prolonged his own personal clean sheet record –
making it nine in a row without conceding.

Right Robin van Persie was also steadily
coming of age, the substitute wasting no time in
making an impression, coolly gliding past Andy
Todd and side-footing home the second.

Right Patrick Vieira needs all his strength to bring the ball away under close attention from David Thompson. Vieira was experiencing one of his toughest afternoons of the season, and he had the bruises to prove it.

Left He'd only been on the pitch eight minutes but Robin van Persie expertly swept home his second, and Arsenal's third of the game, in the final minute. His celebrations were cut short after a collision with Andy Todd.

Right and Far Right **Another
game, another bottle of
champagne for Robert Pires,
while Freddie Ljungberg, who
always seems to leave his
mark at the Millennium
Stadium, signs his portrait
hanging in the stadium's
tunnel area.**

0 ARSENAL
0 MANCHESTER UNITED

**ARSENAL WON 5–4
ON PENALTIES**

Manchester United: van Nistelrooy scored, Scholes saved, Ronaldo scored, Rooney scored, Keane scored

Arsenal: Lauren scored, Ljungberg scored, van Persie scored, Cole scored, Vieira scored

The two most successful clubs in the history of the competition come head-to-head at the Millennium Stadium in a repeat of the 1979 Final. Arsenal, who had won the right to wear the traditional red and white strip, were cheered on by an army of travelling supporters, who were by now becoming used to the surroundings of the Welsh capital.

ARSENAL

1 Jens LEHMANN   12 LAUREN   28 Kolo TOURE   20 Philippe SENDEROS   3 Ashley COLE   15 Francesc FABREGAS   4 Patrick VIEIRA   19 GILBERTO   7 Robert PIRES   10 Dennis BERGKAMP   9 José Antonio REYES   Substitutes   24 Manuel ALMUNIA   23 Sol CAMPBELL   17 EDU (Gilberto) 105   11 Robin VAN PERSIE (Fabregas) 86   8 Fredrik LJUNGBERG (Bergkamp) 65

MANCHESTER UNITED

13 Roy CARROLL   6 Wes BROWN   5 Rio FERDINAND   27 Mikael SILVESTRE   22 John O'SHEA   24 Darren FLETCHER   16 Roy KEANE   18 Paul SCHOLES   7 Cristiano RONALDO   10 Ruud VAN NISTELROOY   8 Wayne ROONEY   Substitutes   1 Tim HOWARD   2 Gary NEVILLE   14 Alan SMITH   25 Quinton FORTUNE (O'Shea) 77   11 Ryan GIGGS (Fletcher) 91

Arsenal 0   Manchester United 0   105

Above Roy Keane and Robert Pires go toe-to-toe as neither side is prepared to concede the initiative in the opening exchanges.

Deprived the services of Golden Boot winner Thierry Henry for the Final, Arsène Wenger reshuffled his line-up and the battle for midfield supremacy proved to be a crucial factor.

Above Gilberto, such a vital cog in the Arsenal machine, turns away from Paul Scholes while Arsène Wenger conveys instructions from the technical area.

Above **A five-man defensive wall is set up by goalkeeper Jens Lehmann as Arsenal prepare to face another Cristiano Ronaldo free-kick.**

The Gunners found themselves under the cosh for much of the game, and were grateful on more than one occasion for the saves of Lehmann – Arsenal's outstanding player on the day.

Below **Patrick Vieira, once again the man for the big occasion, seems unflustered as he finds himself surrounded by a trio of United players.**

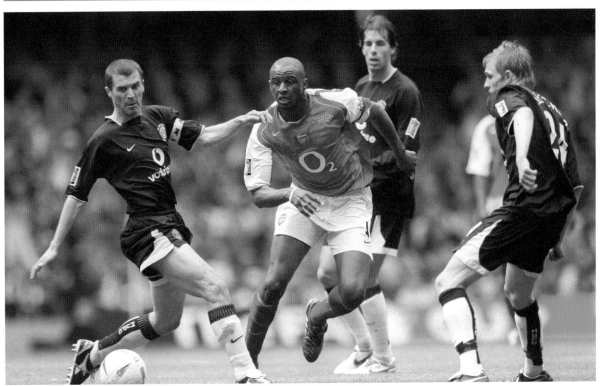

Left Robin van Persie's inch-perfect kick, the first ever penalty of his senior career, was typical of the Gunners' efforts from 12 yards. Lauren, Freddie Ljungberg and Ashley Cole were also spot-on, meaning Jens Lehmann's save from Paul Scholes (far left) allowed Patrick Vieira (below) the chance to win the Cup with the very last kick of the season, and he duly swept the ball past Roy Carroll.

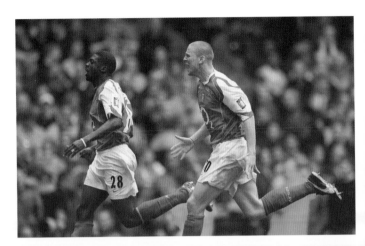

Left and Below With the Cup regained it's time for the celebrations to begin. Kolo Toure and Philippe Senderos lead the charge from the centre-circle to congratulate Patrick Vieira after his decisive penalty. Vieira then becomes the last captain to lift the FA Cup at the Millennium Stadium in front of a spectacular red and white ticker-tape backdrop.

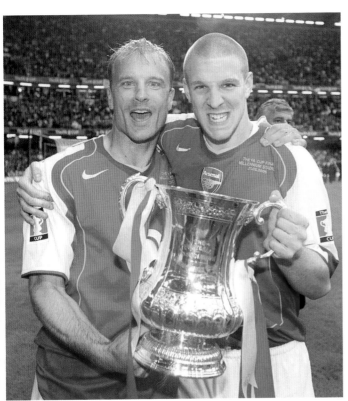

Right **Freddie Ljungberg, Robert Pires, Patrick Vieira, Cesc Fabregas and Dennis Bergkamp** begin the lap of honour with the trophy. It's Arsenal's tenth FA Cup success, and the third in the past four seasons.

Left **Kolo Toure and Robert Pires relax back in their Cup Final suits with the prize for a season's hard work.**

Below **A synchronised 'splash down' on the Millennium Stadium grass – a playing area on which the Gunners have felt so at home over the past five years.**

THE ONES THAT GOT AWAY

2000/01

Third Round Brunton Park	0	**CARLISLE UNITED**
2000/01 6 January 2001	1	**ARSENAL** Wiltord 22

CARLISLE UNITED

22 Matt **GLENNON** 2 Mark **BIRCH** 18 Tony **HEMMINGS**
4 Stuart **WHITEHEAD** 19 Mark **WINSTANLEY**
6 Julian **DARBY** 8 Steve **SOLEY** 16 Richard **PROKAS**
7 Scott **DOBIE** 9 Ian **STEVENS** 15 Gordon **CONNELLY**
Substitutes 10 Carl **HEGGS** (Darby) 53
11 Stephen **HALLIDAY** (Stevens) 69 27 Adam **THWAITES**
(Hemmings) 86 14 John **HORE** 31 John **INGLIS**

ARSENAL

13 Alex **MANNINGER** 2 Lee **DIXON** 3 Igors **STEPANOVS**
23 Nelson **VIVAS** 29 Ashley **COLE** 8 Fredrik **LJUNGBERG**
4 Patrick **VIEIRA** 15 Ray **PARLOUR** 7 Robert **PIRES**
10 Dennis **BERGKAMP** 11 Sylvain **WILTORD** Substitutes
16 **SILVINHO** (Ljungberg) 76 21 Tomas **DANILEVICIUS**
(Wiltord) 81 19 Stefan **MALZ** (Cole) 85 42 John **HALLS**
24 John **LUKIC**

Fourth Round Loftus Road	0	**QUEENS PARK RANGERS**
2000/01 27 January 2001	6	**ARSENAL** Plummer og 32, Wiltord 33, 56, Rose og 49, Pires 58, Bergkamp

QUEENS PARK RANGERS

1 Ludek **MIKLOSKO** 22 Jermaine **DARLINGTON**
3 Ian **BARACLOUGH** 17 Chris **PLUMMER** 24 Mark **PERRY**
18 Clarke **CARLISLE** 21 Richard **LANGLEY**
8 Gavin **PEACOCK** 28 Peter **CROUCH** 12 Matthew **ROSE**
11 Chris **KIWOMYA** Substitutes 10 Karl **CONNOLLY** (Perry)
45 31 Sammy **KOEJOE** (Plummer) 45 9 Michel **NGONGE**
(Koejoe) 72 4 Stephen **MORROW** 13 Lee **HARPER**

ARSENAL

1 David **SEAMAN** 2 Lee **DIXON** 3 Igors **STEPANOVS**
6 Tony **ADAMS** 29 Ashley **COLE** 12 **LAUREN**
4 Patrick **VIEIRA** 15 Ray **PARLOUR** 7 Robert **PIRES**
10 Dennis **BERGKAMP** 11 Sylvain **WILTORD** Substitutes
18 Gilles **GRIMANDI** (Lauren) 67 19 Stefan **MALZ**
(Pires) 75 23 Nelson **VIVAS** (Vieira) 79 14 Thierry **HENRY**
13 Alex **MANNINGER**

3 ARSENAL Henry 52 (pen), Wiltord 74, 85
1 CHELSEA Hasselbaink 62

ARSENAL

1 David **SEAMAN** 2 Lee **DIXON** 3 Igors **STEPANOVS**
22 Oleg **LUZHNY** 29 Ashley **COLE** 12 **LAUREN**
4 Patrick **VIEIRA** 8 Fredrik **LJUNGBERG** 7 Robert **PIRES**
10 Dennis **BERGKAMP** 14 Thierry **HENRY** Substitutes
11 Sylvain **WILTORD** (Pires) 69 23 Nelson **VIVAS**
(Bergkamp) 81 25 **KANU** 19 Stefan **MALZ**
13 Alex **MANNINGER**

CHELSEA

23 Carlo **CUDICINI** 17 Albert **FERRER** 3 Celestine
BABAYARO 10 Slavisa **JOKANOVIC** 26 John **TERRY**
6 Marcel **DESAILLY** 8 Gustavo **POYET**
24 Sam Dalla **BONA** 9 Jimmy Floyd **HASSELBAINK**
25 Gianfranco **ZOLA** 11 Dennis **WISE** Substitutes
22 Eidur **GUDJOHNSEN** (Bona) 46 30 Jesper
GRONKJAER (Zola) 46 12 Mario **STANIC** (Ferrer) 83
5 Frank **LEBOEUF** 1 Ed **DE GOEY**

Above and Right **Sylvain Wiltord maintains his record of scoring in
every round with a brace to kill off Chelsea at Highbury. Lauren
celebrates with Thierry Henry after the Frenchman's successful
penalty conversion gave Arsenal a 52nd-minute lead.**

Sixth Round Highbury
2000/01 10 March 2001

3 ARSENAL Wiltord 2, Adams 5, Pires 36
0 BLACKBURN ROVERS

ARSENAL

1 David **SEAMAN**   2 Lee **DIXON**   6 Tony **ADAMS**
22 Oleg **LUZHNY**   29 Ashley **COLE**   12 **LAUREN**
18 Gilles **GRIMANDI**   8 Fredrik **LJUNGBERG**
7 Robert **PIRES**   10 Dennis **BERGKAMP**
11 Sylvain **WILTORD**   Substitutes   16 **SILVINHO**
(Ljungberg) 65   4 Patrick **VIEIRA** (Pires) 69
14 Thierry **HENRY** (Bergkamp) 69   23 Nelson **VIVAS**
13 Alex **MANNINGER**

BLACKBURN ROVERS

32 Brad **FRIEDEL**   4 Jason **McATEER**   23 Alan **MAHON**
2 John **CURTIS**   21 Henning **BERG**   28 Martin **TAYLOR**
7 Garry **FLITCROFT**   22 Eyal **BERKOVIC**   17 Marcus **BENT**
9 Mark **HUGHES**   8 David **DUNN**   Substitutes
5 Stig Inge **BJORNEBYE** (Mahon) 45   11 Damien **DUFF**
(Berkovic) 45   15 Matt **JANSEN** (Hughes) 61
10 Craig **HIGNETT**   13 Alan **KELLY**

Semi-Final Old Trafford
2000/01 8 April 2001

2 ARSENAL Vieira 33, Pires 74
1 TOTTENHAM HOTSPUR Doherty 14

ARSENAL

1 David **SEAMAN**   2 Lee **DIXON**   6 Tony **ADAMS**
5 Martin **KEOWN**   16 **SILVINHO**   12 **LAUREN**
4 Patrick **VIEIRA**   15 Ray **PARLOUR**   7 Robert **PIRES**
14 Thierry **HENRY**   11 Sylvain **WILTORD**   Substitutes
8 Fredrik **LJUNGBERG** (Pires) 77   29 Ashley **COLE**
(Wiltord) 89   25 **KANU**   22 Oleg **LUZHNY**
13 Alex **MANNINGER**

TOTTENHAM HOTSPUR

13 Neil **SULLIVAN**   2 Stephen **CARR**   21 Luke **YOUNG**
12 Gary **DOHERTY**   5 Sol **CAMPBELL**   6 Chris **PERRY**
8 Tim **SHERWOOD**   10 Steffen **IVERSEN**
11 Sergei **REBROV**   9 Les **FERDINAND**
25 Stephen **CLEMENCE**   Substitutes   26 Ledley **KING**
(Campbell) 38   17 Oyvind **LEONHARDSEN** (Ferdinand) 56
31 Alton **THELWELL** (Clemence) 79   15 Willem **KORSTEN**
1 Ian **WALKER**

Above **The delight is obvious as Patrick Vieira celebrates levelling against Tottenham in the Semi-Final at Old Trafford. With just over 15 minutes remaining Robert Pires scored yet again against Spurs to confirm the win, and the passage through to the first ever FA Cup Final to be held outside England. The one-goal margin of victory masked the superiority Arsenal enjoyed over their North London rivals on the afternoon.**

| Final Millennium Stadium | **1** | **ARSENAL** Ljungberg 72 |
| 2000/01 12 May 2001 | **2** | **LIVERPOOL** Owen 83, 88 |

ARSENAL

1 David **SEAMAN** 2 Lee **DIXON** 6 Tony **ADAMS**
5 Martin **KEOWN** 29 Ashley **COLE** 8 Fredrik **LJUNGBERG**
4 Patrick **VIEIRA** 18 Gilles **GRIMANDI** 7 Robert **PIRES**
14 Thierry **HENRY** 11 Sylvain **WILTORD** Substitutes
15 Ray **PARLOUR** (Wiltord) 76 25 **KANU** (Ljungberg) 85
10 Dennis **BERGKAMP** (Dixon) 89 12 **LAUREN**
13 Alex **MANNINGER**

LIVERPOOL

1 Sander **WESTERVELD** 6 Markus **BABBEL**
23 Jamie **CARRAGHER** 16 Dietmar **HAMMAN**
2 Stephane **HENCHOZ** 12 Sami **HYYPIA**
13 Danny **MURPHY** 17 Steven **GERRARD**
8 Emile **HESKEY** 10 Michael **OWEN** 7 Vladimir **SMICER**
Substitutes 21 Gary **McALLISTER** (Hamman) 60
15 Patrik **BERGER** (Murphy) 77 9 Robbie **FOWLER**
(Smicer) 77 27 Gregory **VIGNAL** 19 Pegguy **ARPHEXAD**

Third Round Elland Road
2003/04 4 January 2004

1 **LEEDS UNITED** Viduka 8
4 **ARSENAL** Henry 26, Edu 32, Pires 87, Toure 90

LEEDS UNITED

1 Paul **ROBINSON**   34 Frazer **RICHARDSON**
22 Michael **DUBERRY**   36 Matthew **KILGALLON**   3 Ian **HARTE**
21 Dominic **MATTEO**   17 Alan **SMITH**   19 Eirik **BAKKE**
23 David **BATTY**   38 James **MILNER**   9 Mark **VIDUKA**
Substitutes   40 Scott **CARSON**   24 Salomon **OLEMBE**
20 Seth **JOHNSON**   10 Lamine **SAKHO** (Bakke) 70
25 Aaron **LENNON** (Milner) 84

ARSENAL

1 Jens **LEHMANN**   12 **LAUREN**   5 Martin **KEOWN**
23 Sol **CAMPBELL**   3 Ashley **COLE**   8 Fredrik **LJUNGBERG**
19 **GILBERTO**   4 Patrick **VIEIRA**   17 **EDU**   25 **KANU**
14 Thierry **HENRY**   Substitutes   24 Rami **SHAABAN**
28 Kolo **TOURE** (Ljungberg) 81   15 Ray **PARLOUR** (Edu) 81
7 Robert **PIRES** (Kanu) 81   37 David **BENTLEY**

4 ARSENAL Bergkamp 19, Ljungberg 28, 68, Bentley 90
1 MIDDLESBROUGH Job 23

ARSENAL

1 Jens **LEHMANN** 12 **LAUREN** 28 Kolo **TOURE**
23 Sol **CAMPBELL** 3 Ashley **COLE** 15 Ray **PARLOUR**
4 Patrick **VIEIRA** 17 **EDU** 7 Robert **PIRES**
8 Fredrik **LJUNGBERG** 10 Dennis **BERGKAMP**
Substitutes 33 Graham **STACK** 5 Martin **KEOWN**
22 Gael **CLICHY** (Vieira) 75 37 David **BENTLEY**
(Bergkamp) 84 54 Quincy **OWUSU-ABEYIE**

MIDDLESBROUGH

1 Mark **SCHWARZER** 15 Danny **MILLS** 5 Chris **RIGGOTT**
3 Franck **QUEUDRUE** 21 Stuart **PARNABY**
14 Gaizka **MENDIETA** 7 George **BOATENG**
19 Stewart **DOWNING** 27 Boudewijn **ZENDEN**
14 Joseph-Desire **JOB** 17 Michael **RICKETTS**
Substitutes 35 Bradley **JONES** 24 Andrew **DAVIES**
10 **JUNINHO** (Job) 73 8 Szilard **NEMETH** (Downing) 73
9 Massimo **MACCARONE** (Ricketts) 73

Above **David Bentley** celebrates his first goal for the Club – a sublime lob to complete the 4–1 win over Middlesbrough.

Fifth Round Highbury	**2**	**ARSENAL**	Reyes 55, 61
2003/04 15 February 2004	**1**	**CHELSEA**	Mutu 40

ARSENAL

1 Jens **LEHMANN** 12 **LAUREN** 28 Kolo **TOURE**
23 Sol **CAMPBELL** 3 Ashley **COLE** 15 Ray **PARLOUR**
19 **GILBERTO** 4 Patrick **VIEIRA** 7 Robert **PIRES**
10 Dennis **BERGKAMP** 9 José Antonio **REYES**
Substitutes 33 Graham **STACK** 18 Pascal **CYGAN**
22 Gael **CLICHY** (Reyes) 82 17 **EDU** (Parlour) 51
37 David **BENTLEY**

CHELSEA

23 Carlo **CUDICINI** 15 Mario **MELCHIOT**
13 William **GALLAS** 26 John **TERRY** 18 Wayne **BRIDGE**
19 Scott **PARKER** 4 Claude **MAKELELE**
8 Frank **LAMPARD** 30 Jesper **GRONKJAER**
7 Adrian **MUTU** 9 Jimmy-Floyd **HASSELBAINK**
Substitutes 34 Neil **SULLIVAN** (Cudicini) 60
29 Robert **HUTH** 10 Joe **COLE** (Gronkjaer) 69
22 Eidur **GUDJOHNSEN** (Mutu) 64 21 Hernan **CRESPO**

Above **Spaniard José Antonio Reyes chooses the perfect moment to score his first goals for the Club. He smashed home an unstoppable equaliser, then six minutes later netted a fine winner as, for the fourth consecutive season, Arsenal sent London rivals Chelsea tumbling out of the FA Cup.**

Sixth Round Fratton Park
2003/04 6 March 2004

1 PORTSMOUTH Sheringham 90
5 ARSENAL Henry 25, 50, Ljungberg 43, 57, Toure 45

PORTSMOUTH

1 Shaka **HISLOP** 2 Linvoy **PRIMUS** 34 Petri **PASANEN**
6 Arjan **DE ZEEUW** 30 Alexei **SMERTIN**
11 Nigel **QUASHIE** 15 Amdy **FAYE** 39 Eyal **BERKOVIC**
14 Matthew **TAYLOR** 20 Ayegbeni **YAKUBU**
37 Ivica **MORNAR** Substitutes 25 Harald **WAPENAAR**
7 Kevin **HARPER** 19 Steve **STONE** (Berkovic) 46
22 Richard **HUGHES** (Quashie) 70
10 Teddy **SHERINGHAM** (Mornar) 77

ARSENAL

1 Jens **LEHMANN** 12 **LAUREN** 28 Kolo **TOURE**
23 Sol **CAMPBELL** 3 Ashley **COLE** 8 Fredrik **LJUNGBERG**
4 Patrick **VIEIRA** 17 **EDU** 19 **GILBERTO**
14 Thierry **HENRY** 9 José Antonio **REYES**
Substitutes 13 Stuart **TAYLOR** 18 Pascal **CYGAN**
22 Gael **CLICHY** (Vieira) 72 37 David **BENTLEY**
(Ljungberg) 72 25 **KANU** (Henry) 72

The Gunners' performance in the FA Cup Quarter-Final was appreciated by home and away fans alike. The Fratton Park faithful gave Arsène Wenger's team a standing ovation at half-time and full-time after witnessing a devastating performance of free-flowing attacking football.

Semi-Final Villa Park
2003/04 3 April 2004

0 ARSENAL
1 MANCHESTER UNITED Scholes 32

ARSENAL

1 Jens **LEHMANN** 12 **LAUREN** 28 Kolo **TOURE**
23 Sol **CAMPBELL** 22 Gael **CLICHY** 8 Fredrik **LJUNGBERG**
4 Patrick **VIEIRA** 17 **EDU** 7 Robert **PIRES**
10 Dennis **BERGKAMP** 30 Jeremie **ALIADIERE**
Substitutes 33 Graham **STACK** 5 Martin **KEOWN**
25 **KANU** (Edu) 76 9 José Antonio **REYES** (Aliadiere) 57
14 Thierry **HENRY** (Pires) 58

MANCHESTER UNITED

13 Roy **CARROLL** 2 Gary **NEVILLE** 6 Wes **BROWN**
27 Mikael **SILVESTRE** 22 John **O'SHEA**
7 Cristiano **RONALDO** 16 Roy **KEANE**
24 Darren **FLETCHER** 18 Paul **SCHOLES**
11 Ryan **GIGGS** 20 Ole Gunnar **SOLSKJAER**
Substitutes 14 Tim **HOWARD** 3 Phil **NEVILLE**
(Solskjaer) 75 19 Eric **DJEMBA-DJEMBA** 8 Nicky **BUTT**
12 David **BELLION** (Ronaldo) 84

ARSENAL AND THE FA CUP

THE FACTS

Arsenal scored the latest ever goal in an FA Cup Final in the 1993 Final against Sheffield Wednesday. In the final minute of extra-time in the replay (the 210th minute of the tie) Andy Linighan headed home from a corner to give Arsenal the Cup with a 2–1 win at Wembley.

At the other end of the spectrum, Alan Sunderland's strike for Arsenal after just 13 seconds in the Semi-Final second replay against Liverpool in 1980 was the fastest ever FA Cup goal at the time.

David Jack became the first player to feature in FA Cup Finals for two different clubs when playing for Arsenal in the 1930 Final against Huddersfield. He had previously played in the Final for Bolton Wanderers, and indeed scored the first ever Cup Final goal at Wembley in 1923.

Brian Talbot became the first player to win back-to-back FA Cup Finals when he helped Arsenal beat Manchester United 3–2 in 1979. The previous year he was part of the Ipswich Town side which beat Arsenal 1–0 in the Final.

Arsenal competed in, and won, the first ever 'indoor' FA Cup Final. Due to heavy rain, the roof on the Millennium Stadium was closed for the entire 2003 Final against Southampton.

Arsène Wenger is the only Arsenal boss to have won more than one FA Cup Final. His current tally of four puts him second in the all-time list of most successful managers in the competition.

The first ever FA Cup Final to be broadcast by the BBC was the 1927 Final between Arsenal and Cardiff, which the Welsh side won 1–0.

The 1950 FA Cup Final against Liverpool saw Arsenal wear an away strip for the first time. Both teams abandoned their usual red, and the Gunners went for a gold shirt with white collars and shorts.

In 1950 Arsenal became the first club to win the FA Cup without leaving London during the entire run.

Jointly with Manchester United, Arsenal hold the record for the most appearances in the FA Cup Final with 17.

Arsène Wenger has led Arsenal to the last five successive FA Cup Semi-Finals.

The Gunners' biggest win in the FA Cup came in 1893 when they beat Ashford United 12–0 at home in the First Qualifying Round. It remains the Club's biggest ever win in any competition (joint with 12–0 league win over Loughborough Town in 1900).

The Club's first ever FA Cup tie, before they were a league side, ended in an 11–0 victory over Lyndhurst in 1889 when they were known as Royal Arsenal.

Arsenal have won ten FA Cups, one behind Manchester United who have won the most, but two ahead of Tottenham who are third in the list with eight successes.

José Antonio Reyes is only the second player ever to be sent off in an FA Cup Final following Kevin Moran in 1985.

Arsenal have lost just one of their last 26 FA Cup fixtures (the 2004 Semi-Final to Manchester United).

Arsenal haven't lost at home in the FA Cup since Leeds won 1–0 at Highbury in the Fourth Round on 4 February 1997 – a run of 20 fixtures.

Patrick Vieira has appeared in eight FA Cup Semi-Finals for Arsenal, including the replay in 1999.

Arsenal remained unbeaten for 18 consecutive FA Cup matches between 2001 and 2004 – a post-war record.

The penalty shoot-out in the 2005 FA Cup Final was the first time the Cup had ever been decided that way.

Arsenal hold the record for most appearances in the FA Cup Semi-Finals with 25.

Pat Rice, either as a player or Assistant Manager, has been to ten FA Cup Finals with Arsenal.

Arsenal's all-time leading scorer in the FA Cup is Cliff Bastin, who scored 26 goals in 42 appearances between 1929 and 1939.

FA CUP RECORD THIS MILLENNIUM

Season	Pld	W	D	L	F	A
2004/2005	7	6	1	0	9	2
2003/2004	5	4	0	1	15	5
2002/2003	7	6	1	0	16	4
2001/2002	7	6	1	0	17	5
2000/2001	6	5	0	1	16	4
	32	27	3	2	73	20

THE MILLENNIUM MEN

Arsenal appearances and goals in the FA Cup from 2000 to 2005
+ = substitutes, (goals in brackets)

Player	Apps	+Sub	(Goals)
Patrick Vieira	28	+1	(2)
Lauren	22		(2)
Robert Pires	21	+6	(8)
Fredrik Ljungberg	21	+3	(10)
Ashley Cole	19	+1	
Sol Campbell	18		(2)
Dennis Bergkamp	17	+5	(7)
Sylvain Wiltord	14	+6	(10)
Edu	13	+4	(3)
Ray Parlour	13	+4	(2)
Thierry Henry	12	+6	(6)
Kolo Toure	12	+4	(2)
Martin Keown	11	+1	
David Seaman	11		
Jens Lehmann	10		
Lee Dixon	8	+2	
José Antonio Reyes	8	+1	(3)
Oleg Luzhny	8		
Francis Jeffers	7	+1	(3)
Tony Adams	7		(2)
Gael Clichy	6	+3	
Gilberto	6	+2	
Philippe Senderos	6		
Kanu	5	+5	(2)
Giovanni van Bronckhorst	5	+2	
Richard Wright	5		
Francesc Fabregas	4	+2	
Pascal Cygan	4	+1	
Mathieu Flamini	4		
Igors Stepanovs	4		
Gilles Grimandi	3	+4	
Robin van Persie	3	+2	(3)
Emmanuel Eboue	3		
Stuart Taylor	3		
Manuel Almunia	2		
Jeremie Aliadiere	1	+2	
Silvinho	1	+2	
Nelson Vivas	1	+2	
Matthew Upson	1	+1	
Juan	1		
Arturo Lupoli	1		
Alex Manninger	1		
Jermaine Pennant	1		
Sebastian Svard	1		
David Bentley		+3	(1)
Stefan Malz		+2	
Quincy Owusu-Abeyie		+2	
Tomas Danilevicius		+1	
Justin Hoyte		+1	
Own goals			(5)

FINAL COUNTDOWN

Arsenal's complete FA Cup Final record:

23 April 1927
Cardiff City 1   Arsenal 0
D Lewis, T Parker, A Kennedy, A Baker,
J Butler, R John, J Hulme, C Buchan, J Brain,
W Blyth, S Hoar
Manager: Herbert Chapman
Wembley (Att: 91,206)

26 April 1930
Arsenal 2   Huddersfield Town 0
(Lambert, James)
C Preedy, T Parker, E Hapgood, A Baker,
W Seddon, R John, J Hulme, D Jack,
J Lambert, A James, C Bastin
Manager: Herbert Chapman
Wembley (Att: 92,486)

23 April 1932
Newcastle United 2   Arsenal 1
(John)
F Moss, T Parker, E Hapgood, C Jones,
H Roberts, G Male, J Hulme, D Jack, J Lambert,
C Bastin, R John
Manager: Herbert Chapman
Wembley (Att: 92,298)

25 April 1936
Arsenal 1   Sheffield United 0
(Drake)
A Wilson, G Male, E Hapgood, W Crayston,
H Roberts, W Copping, J Hulme, R Bowden,
E Drake, A James, C Bastin
Manager: George Allison
Wembley (Att: 93,384)

29 April 1950
Arsenal 2   Liverpool 0
(Lewis 2)
G Swindin, L Scott, W Barnes, A Forbes,
L Compton, J Mercer, F Cox, J Logie, P Goring,
R Lewis, D Compton
Manager: Tom Whittaker
Wembley (Att: 100,000)

3 May 1952
Newcastle United 1   Arsenal 0
G Swindin, W Barnes, L Smith, A Forbes,
R Daniel, J Mercer, F Cox, J Logie, C Holton,
D Lishman, D Roper
Manager: Tom Whittaker
Wembley (Att: 100,000)

8 May 1971

Arsenal 2   Liverpool 1 (aet)

(Kelly, George)

B Wilson, P Rice, R McNab, P Storey (E Kelly),
F McLintock, P Simpson, G Armstrong,
G Graham, J Radford, R Kennedy, C George
Manager: Bertie Mee
Wembley (Att: 100,000)

6 May 1972

Leeds United 1   Arsenal 0

G Barnett, P Rice, R McNab, P Storey,
F McLintock, P Simpson, G Armstrong, A Ball,
C George, J Radford (R Kennedy), G Graham
Manager: Bertie Mee
Wembley (Att: 100,000)

6 May 1978

Ipswich Town 1   Arsenal 0

P Jennings, P Rice, S Nelson, D Price,
D O'Leary, W Young, L Brady (G Rix),
A Sunderland, M MacDonald, F Stapleton,
A Hudson
Manager: Terry Neill
Wembley (Att: 100,000)

12 May 1979

Arsenal 3   Manchester United 2 (aet)

(Talbot, Stapleton, Sunderland)

P Jennings, P Rice, S Nelson, B Talbot,
D O'Leary, W Young, L Brady, A Sunderland,
F Stapleton, D Price (S Walford), G Rix
Manager: Terry Neill
Wembley (Att: 100,000)

10 May 1980

West Ham United 1   Arsenal 0

P Jennings, P Rice, J Devine (S Nelson),
B Talbot, D O'Leary, W Young, L Brady,
A Sunderland, F Stapleton, D Price, G Rix
Manager: Terry Neill
Wembley (Att: 100,000)

15 May 1993

Arsenal 1   Sheffield Wednesday 1

(Wright)

D Seaman, L Dixon, N Winterburn, P Davis,
A Linighan, T Adams, J Jensen, I Wright
(D O'Leary), K Campbell, P Merson, R Parlour
(A Smith)
Manager: George Graham
Wembley (Att: 79,347)

20 May 1993 (replay)

Arsenal 2   Sheffield Wednesday 1 (aet)

(Wright, Linighan)

D Seaman, L Dixon, N Winterburn, P Davis,
A Linighan, T Adams, J Jensen, I Wright
(D O'Leary), A Smith, P Merson, K Campbell
Manager: George Graham
Wembley (Att: 62,267)

16 May 1998

Arsenal 2   Newcastle United 0

(Overmars, Anelka)

D Seaman, L Dixon, N Winterburn, P Vieira,
T Adams, N Anelka, M Overmars, M Keown,
R Parlour, E Petit, C Wreh (D Platt)
Manager: Arsène Wenger
Wembley (Att: 79,183)

12 May 2001

Liverpool 2   Arsenal 1

(Ljungberg)

D Seaman, L Dixon (D Bergkamp), A Cole,
P Vieira, M Keown, T Adams, R Pires,
F Ljungberg (Kanu), S Wiltord (R Parlour),
T Henry, G Grimandi
Manager: Arsène Wenger
Millennium Stadium, Cardiff (Att: 72,500)

4 May 2002

Arsenal 2   Chelsea 0

(Ljungberg, Parlour)

D Seaman, Lauren, A Cole, T Adams,
S Campbell, P Vieira, R Parlour, F Ljungberg,
D Bergkamp (Edu), S Wiltord (M Keown),
T Henry (Kanu)
Manager: Arsène Wenger
Millennium Stadium, Cardiff (Att: 73,963)

17 May 2003

Arsenal 1   Southampton 0

(Pires)

D Seaman, Lauren, M Keown, O Luzhny,
A Cole, R Pires, R Parlour, Gilberto,
F Ljungberg, T Henry, D Bergkamp (S Wiltord)
Manager: Arsène Wenger
Millennium Stadium, Cardiff (Att: 73,726)

21 May 2005

Arsenal 0   Manchester United 0 (aet)

(Arsenal won 5–4 on penalties)

J Lehmann, Lauren, P Senderos, K Toure,
A Cole, R Pires (Edu), F Fabregas
(R van Persie), P Vieira, Gilberto, JA Reyes,
D Bergkamp (F Ljungberg)
Manager: Arsène Wenger
Millennium Stadium, Cardiff (Att: 71,876)

OVERALL RECORD IN FINALS

P	W	D	L	F	A
18	10	1	7	20	14